Critical Reception of *As Close As I Can Get*

Timothy Donohue's poems sizzle with insights and vibrate with recognitions and second-guesses. He knows how to make them interrogate their own medium, language, with gratifying results. This collection, spanning years, gives us a gift to treasure and explore, a book of remarkable strength and discipline.

—David Young, author of
Field of Light and Shadow: Selected and New Poems
(Newly Expanded Paperback Edition)

By choosing to title the longest poem in this volume "The Book of Revelation," you begin to see the reflective and refractive lens that Donohue brings to his task as a poet. The word "revelation," meaning an unveiling, a revealing—has a psychological as well as a theological history of use. As a reader, I can participate in the poet's discoveries: "what's severed can itch; can stub its invisible toe" and then the paradox: "what's gone remains. But what remains/isn't always so true/like the word 'know'/or the arc of this poem." When I read these and other lines in *As Close As I Can Get*, I feel something in me begin to knit. Perhaps it is the healing balm of irony itself so elegantly rendered in the language only poets can utter.

—Dennis Patrick Slattery, PhD., author of
Just Below the Water Line: Selected Poems and
The Way of Myth: Stories' Subtle Wisdom

Timothy Donohue's latest book of poetry is a gift, a gift of stunning, memorable poetry, comprising the best of previous volumes combined with a generous portion of new offerings. One of the most captivating features of Donohue's poetry is how easy he makes it look. Don't be fooled, however. He works meticulously, honing and polishing, until every facet of each gem gets as close to perfection as possible. His poems are like probes sent out into a world that lies just beyond the borders of our everyday experiences and perceptions. They probe the secrets and puzzles of language, poetry, and existence. They even probe the mysteries of their own workings. Most of all, they probe us, provoke us, and invite us to sense the joy and wonder of being sojourners in this vexing, flawed, and glorious life.

—Donald Carlson, PhD, author of
*Tweeting Dante: One Hundred Days of Tweets
from Dante's Divine Comedy*

This volume's most obvious masterpiece, "The Book of Revelation," is an epic of love deferred and disappointment made flesh, set to the ticking of mortality's clock, and embedded in a Midwestern landscape of forests, factories, and a lake as big as an ocean. But there is much more here: mysteries, revelations, and hints of grace, underlined by a sly wit. A bountiful collection.

—David Barbour,
New York Drama Critics' Circle,
Editor-In-Chief *Lighting &Sound America*

AS CLOSE AS I CAN GET

Selected And New Poems

*To Yehuda —
with love
Tim
10. 17. 22*

TIMOTHY DONOHUE

Cover art, "Eyes on the Canvas" by Timothy Donohue
Cover design by Jennifer Leigh Selig
Author photo by Zoe Friedman Walsh

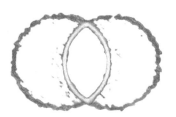

MANDORLA BOOKS
WWW.MANDORLABOOKS.COM

"To me, poetry is somebody standing up, so to speak, and saying, with as little concealment as possible, what it is for him or her to be on earth at this moment."

Galway Kinnell

"The world is so much larger than what people remember."

Susan Sontag

"Sometimes poems aren't literal representations of anything. Sometimes a poem just exists as something else in the universe that you haven't encountered before.

Mark Strand

"I know I'm in a vast parenthesis."

Kenneth Koch

For Mara, who saw invisibilities and stayed.
For Monica, who never gave up looking.
For David Young, who pulled back the curtains.

TABLE OF CONTENTS

Selections From
Road, Frame, Window

Selections From
Invisible

Selections From
Eve And Other Acts Of Defiant Gratitude

New Poems

Selections from
Road, Frame, Window

Like A Hole In The Wind

> "God made everything out of nothing,
> But the nothingness shows through."
> ~Paul Valery

It appears out of nowhere
A there, that's not there
An invisible absence
Like a hole in the wind

Where the bending tree had been
Now there's a broken fence
That buries itself in snowstorms
Who are you to believe?

You perfect making up things on the spot
Conversations without a shared past are preferred
Because you will misplace those moments too
Because all the nouns have names

Because hearing cannot take notes
In mid-air

This is the gyre of memory
The spinning backwards
Until you find the empty part in everything
Until you're sprawled out
In a place made ready for the absent

Where what's expected of you
Is more invisible
Than nothing at all

Just Like A Movie

We don't remember the beginning
The darkness turning to light, the scream
The masked men welcoming you to their hangout
But we'll remember the ending
The light fading to black
The hushed voices saying
It's OK, it's OK to go
To leave out of here
To be on your way to forever…
The credits roll
They sweep around the seats
A boy in an oversized red jacket
Says have a nice day
The doors open
The light's blinding

20 Footnotes Found In A Text On Blood

1.
Whatever is said from the heart
is irreversible. It is the poem
as human being. Please understand
what happens. Listen to your blood.

2.
I drink more coffee per day
than anyone still alive.
As lies go, it's true.

3.
Nothing is as useless, hopeless
and necessary in the exact same
moment as language.

4.
Getting into your thirties,
you finally learn something
about this word "possible".

5.
Never paying attention to titles,
you wake up married to the vice-
president of lust. The one who
does nothing, and does it very well.
The one that will be reelected.

6.
At 24, I was in the worst fight
of my life. Lost consciousness.
Saw stars. Crawled looking for

my glasses to see them better.

7.
I'm capable of falling in love
with certain types of women
the moment I see them. If I
rise to the occasion, it's
another blood test.

8.
The chemists call it $C8-H10-N4-02$.
At a certain level of circulation,
the world reaches a pitch spectrum
that lets you see anything you want
to hear. Then darkness. Abyss
with a name.

9.
How do we separate the legitimate
from the junk? I don't know…
is the answer. A 100-proof poem
can be detected in the bloodstream;
but you can make up all kinds of
answers…depending on who you're
trying to avoid or impress.

10.
A fool for love. Yes, and a big one.
When I'm "in it", I'll put my foot
in my mouth enough times to chew it into
little pieces. Just to get the other
in the door. Just to vary
my diet of clichés.

11.
"We must grant the poet the first line."
Someone was telling a class somewhere.
And what about two through 4,000?
Or everything that comes after the
first dollop of paint; and all the
notes that come after her opening
chord? No one asked the question.
It gunned my blood.

12.
I'll do something or I'll do nothing.
I don't understand the in between.
I cannot live a life of go between.
"Over" goes only with "do" for me.

13.
Memory, imagination, love, lust
and language pile up in the hollows.
What happens can't be avoided.
There's no bypass, no blood-thinners
for this.

14.
I quit booze years ago. I quit
fighting because I quit booze.
I could quit coffee, cigarettes
and poetry. But that would be
like never taking my pants off.
A solar system of unnamed, seen-
once stars would blink out in
my head; faster than they
already are.

15.
The poem, like television, movies
based on novels and the man who
plays a banjo on a street corner
is not your enemy. It is the lost
sister found weeping inside you;
it is your brother in blood.

16.
Past maximum levels, just before
you find your cot in the abyss
of the confused; the fingers
the toes, the lips and half
a face cool and numb. The heart
starts its descent.

17.
How do we separate the legitimate…?
Some won't take "I don't know"
for an answer. They never will;
because they won't let the poem
speak to just anybody. They make
it sign-in with the secretary
at the office of 100-proof readers.

18.
Being young and getting older
like hypermyopia, acute astigmatism,
lust and love can be dealt with.
We can treat symptoms, make adjustments.
But there is no science for the tone-deaf.
A whole language is lost forever.

19.
Given only one to work with,
somehow we manage to squeeze
many lives through our veins.
Knowing that none of them will
ever really be completed; that
each and every one, like a poem
is eventually abandoned. Left alone.

20.
Though sometimes it's as stupid,
impossible and funny as trying to
study for a blood test, we try.
That's the beauty, we try.

Texas Legend

Between Midland and Odessa
one rusty pond is shaped
like a jackrabbit missing a paw.

Between San Angelo and San Benito
a missionary's black boot
is stuffed with mockingbird skulls.

Between Austin and Houston
an armadillo has its head
painted a metallic orange.

Between Dallas and Fort Worth
there's a tiny silver door
hung with rattlesnake hinges.

Between Bowie and Sherman
a coyote hangs shot in a tree
suspended by a piano wire.

Between Laredo and Zapata
one star is shaped like a bullet
another like a piñata.

Below The Stain

The notebook's
Round stain
Remembers everything:

The blue gin glass
The yellow fingers
The cigarettes

It was Saturday, October, 1975

The hot air was soaked
With the smell of dried
Oak and bois d'arc leaves

Album after album
Music poured through
The apartment

"Beauty must feel like this,"
I wrote in a notebook
Stained by a sweating glass…

Rain poured from a rattling sky
Humid and earth-smelling
The sheets clung to us

Like watery white clay

Using beer for coffee
Sobriety arrived late
That Sunday

Or maybe not at all…
Who knows how things
Really fall below the stain

Daddy's At The Office (I)

I will die.
The man in the office next to me will die.

The building I'm in is eight years old.
It is 1:10 in the afternoon. I'm reading a book.

I am remembering a fact
I once felt about death.

I am writing something in a notebook.
You are reading something else.

It is much later.

I cannot see the man in the office next to me.
He is eating fruit from a peanut butter jar.

I can see him wearing a blue shirt made out of petroleum.
He has one grey athletic shoe on each foot.

He is eating crackers from a sandwich bag.
You are reading this.

You are thinking
About a petroleum-blue shirt.

You are wondering about the name
On the yellow lid of the peanut butter jar.

The balls of cantaloupe.
The thaw of frozen strawberries.

You know what I tell you.
You think what you want.

I hear a man drop a metal spoon.
Hear it scrape around a jar without a lid.

The man in the office next to me
Is scraping bottom.

You think the last two words are too à la mode.
I told you about the fruit.

Now you are doing arithmetic.
I like you very much. I hope you are a woman.

I was smoking and reading a book.
Someone was eating lunch.

I tilted my book on my chest,
I wrote "I will die" in a notebook.

It was 4 December 1987
That's how we met.

Daddy's At The Office (II)

It's much later now.
We all must die.

I hear an empty jar being pushed across a desk.
The room is filled with fruit.

A man in an office next to me.
A jar is being washed in a bathroom.

Empty jar in a brown bag.
Brown bag in a briefcase with accordion sides.

It's 1:37 in the afternoon.
When I was 12, I had a bicycle with golden fenders.

A briefcase was a bookbag.
The valise hung from handlebars. I pedaled away.

That was 289,000 hours ago.
You were somewhere else.

When I was 35, I wrote.
I wrote "I will die" in a notebook.

Perhaps you were doing arithmetic then.
Perhaps you were at your desk eating peanut butter.

Here we have seven offices for six people.
You know what offices look like.

Five people are not here.
You are now in my office.

Now I am reading for you.
Now I am listening to you.

The man in the office next to me is staring at a green screen.
He remembers how much he likes fruit.

He is 59 years old.
His breath is a bouquet of crackers and fruit.

He has no children.
He is not all you see.

In one office there is one ashtray.
I hope you are a woman.

The wind is from the south at ten miles an hour.
The temperature is in the seventies. The sky is blue.

Daddy's At The Office (III)

I entered the building at 11:07 a.m.
Four men were on the roof with brooms dipped in tar.

We are staring at one another now.
We listen to each other's eyes.

There was a machine outside making tar.
Four men with brooms have finished their lunches.

If there was a window in this basement
I would show you this tar.

I was reading a book.
It is 3:09 p.m.

Outside the smell of gasoline and leaves.
Dinosaurs emerged from snow and floated in the air.

You like those last two lines.
I hope you are not stopping there.

I like you very much.
I'm glad all this happened millions of years ago.

Cigarettes and tar float in a blue sky.
Aren't you glad you quit smoking?

The wind has gusted to 16 miles per hour.
A notebook is on my desk.

In 420 hours it will be Christmas Eve.
I am a man with one child.

On Christmas Eve, I will not be here.
The man who told me about his lunch at the Thai restaurant will be gone.

The man is not in the office next to me. It's past five.
I'm not alone. I'm a daughter's father.

I hope you're a woman.
In 420 hours the tar will be dry.

The roof will be empty.

Suit

It's a university
But still I wear a suit.

Like every day was
Business as usual

Or I was burying friends
By the hour.

It's just an old habit
I carry with me

Like a nervous laugh
And a pack of cigarettes…

I spent years
In something called:

Advertising Agency.

In Advertising Agency
Suit was more than fabric

It was the stitch of clothes
That stitched us all together

The copywriter to the account executive
The account executive to the secretary

And all of us, to something called:
Fear of Clients.
Suit was a way of holding hands

Without touching

A way of connecting the dots
Of boozy evenings

With jittery mornings.
Suits seemed to connect everything

Except Saturdays and Sundays.
When we'd lay in our beds, nauseous with fear

And feeling so nude
In our pajamas…

It's a campus
After a rainfall.
I am going to something called:
The Rare Book Room.

I am going to hear the poet
Naomi Shihab Nye.

I am wearing a suit.

The wind smells like green earth.
It is spring.

It will get cold again,
But it is spring.

Students cross wet pavement in all directions
A conversation comes forward

Carried by wind.

Carried by the sweet green earth-smelling wind:

He knows his stuff,
He just doesn't know how to teach it.

Says a beautiful blond girl
In a yellow paisley shirt.

She is more beautiful
Than her boyfriend can possibly understand.

She has more yellow paisley now
Than she will ever have again…

And I want to touch her hand
I want to say: Come.

Come hear this poet with me.

This isn't business
Don't be afraid

It'll get cold again
But it's spring.

Come hear this poet with me
And don't be afraid.

I have not come this far,
In this suit,

To bury you.

A Hundred Kinds Of Sadness

for Y. Y.

There's a stone
Where your voice should be
So now you are with me
As a hundred kinds of sadness

…

There are a hundred kinds of sadness
And I have numbered each one
To bring your disappointment in me forward
And glue myself to your loss

…

February
A long shaft of late winter sunlight
Cuts across the floor and pools
In a last footprint left by a bed

…

Going forward isn't always a good plan
There's a last step to everything
And a hundred kinds of sadness
To everyone

Magician

Take the biggest thing you believe in
Shrink it down to something
Bigger than a pencil
But smaller than a bowl of cereal

Now look out a window:
Good. And again. Good.
Report back to your window in a week—
Everything will be smaller...

Now tell us
(here's the trick):

How many glances
Will it take to break
All these shrunken things
You keep returning to

Selections from
Invisible

Definitions Of Rest

What you hope
Will turn to sleep

A sporting lie
About the bench

What the arm seeks
In airplanes

A calling to
In obituaries

What the weary
Will never get

A symbol of silence
In music

The word the jury
Is waiting for

The opposite
Of bodies in motion

The length of your life
At the beginning of love

The Preferred Embrace

On a sidewalk,
Snow falls between
A man and a woman
Struggling against late December winds—it's obvious
Their separateness is pre-planned
The snowy gap is precise
And irrevocable.

There is no touching now in these lives.
No looking back, nor at each other.
Just a wobbly march forward,
Into more and more invisibility.

What was the word that sawed them in half?
What failures of desire
Would make falling down,
Alone, under a winter sky,

The preferred embrace

Notes From The Last Time I Saw Ferlinghetti

"...there's no there, there."
Gertrude Stein, *Everybody's Autobiography*

Weekend-ending. Runway-runaway
Dallas to San Francisco 1:10 a.m.
And where I'm heading it's 1986,
But it's still yesterday
So much for the times of our life

I have made a mess of my life
Mixed the mess and painted with it
To outline voices in frames of silence
To take the waiting-for, out of wonder
To hear silence, with new ears

Like a poem, and making
That kind of sense, you left
Ferlinghetti in your Texas college town
And headed to his. You see his motel
Room stuttering, repeating itself in his sleep

Forty-five degrees south by southwest
The machine turned, pointing
A wing at Dallas another
At San Francisco. You hear someone
On the ground pointing a finger
At you. Feathers will fly

The flight attendant leans over
Picking up a napkin. You use the word
"Callipygian" for the first time out loud
She smiles, looking backwards

She is happily confused. She will be
Your friend in the sky

Baudelaire said he wrote to
"Find the why of it; to transform pleasure
Into knowledge." I do it differently
There is so much
I don't want to know

Between friendship and love
Comes conversational botany
A kind of plant-talk develops
Between a man and a woman
"Nice day." "Yes. I was tired of the rain"

"I see that bridge we were on"
Says a boy to his dad in the seat ahead
When you turn, it's not there anymore
Your lips taste like a woman's cheekbone
Communication from the neck up

"By definition, the poet must be
An enemy of the State" said Ferlinghetti
Afterward, you drove him to where
He would sleep, perhaps to dream
Against the state of Ramada Inn

Tired and unmemorized
You are up to 30,000 feet
And 36 straight hours
You're slipping deeper
Into ball turret 36B

A fish turns in your stomach
It hears the desert below you
It hears the cacti and it hears
The coyotes below you.

There's a "there" there
It's just that whatever is unclear
Must be so cleared away, it takes the waiting-
For out of wonder. Like hearing silence
With new ears. Or seeing Ferlinghetti
Ten hours before arriving where he wasn't

Thirty years ago

The Poems You Will Never Read

1.
The first poem you will never read
Will be in a magazine
You rarely buy
Because the covers do not satisfy

2.
The second poem you will never read
Will be even better than the first one—
And all you had to do was glance at that book
Left open on the airline seat next to you

3.
And so it goes…
Poetic absences and invisibilities surround you, year after year
But how could you know? You with your avoidance issues
And your deep love of real life

4.
Finally, according to our records,
The fourth, fifteenth and twenty-seventh poems you will
       never read
Were not your fault. You bought the magazines
But the poems that should have been there

Were forced to disappear by others

At A Graveyard By An Orchard

We know how
The slight rounding
Of a high corner
Means the headstone
Has memorized the wind

We can raise a yellow-gold apple at dusk
And trace with a cool finger
Where the sunlight sat for hours

We are much more invisible than that
We are a name halved backwards
A thousand times

Living changes lives
Until who we are
And who we were
Are less known
Than what the wind
And sunlight did
The day these bodies
Were covered with earth

We are all energy and invisibility
We are all someone
We can only imagine

Application Denied

Your application for Sainthood has been denied
There were numerous gaps
In your *History of Listening* section
And your *Essay on Intercessions* was wanting
More disturbing was the complete lack of any metrics
For evaluating your effectiveness in wish-granting
We will keep your application on file for one year
And we encourage you to keep up the good work
In July we will begin accepting applications for Idols
This position may be of some interest to you

Invisible

1.
I stood in line behind a fragrance.
It was you. Your face was invisible,
But it was you.
This was a long time ago.

2.
An electric door kept opening and closing.
Pushing your scent deep inside me,
And urging me to say something clever
To the back of your head.

3.
Inside everyone is a door
They will not open,
And a door they will not close—
Choices must be made.

4.
I should have made you laugh.
Said some nonsense about
Your oolong tea or the candy bar
With the same name as your father

But I remained invisible.

What It's About

I hand you a poem
You say, "what's it about?"

This is what it's about

"I know" you say
But how did you get this?
"You mean the poem?"

"Yes, of course I mean the poem"
That's what I'm asking
Oh, I don't know that

But this is about you
About you asking
What the poem is "about"

About is always
Exactly the same thing
"What's that?"

The thing you haven't read yet

Lives In A Coma

1.
Sometimes I wonder
If there was another way,
An ending we might have missed...
It was late morning
It was the end of summer
Cars came infrequently past that motel
A dog barked
Then silence would return,
Coating our lips
And closing our eyes

2.
We played hooky from real love for so long
We lied about our whereabouts so often
Sometimes we forgot our real names...
Everything outside that room was always boiled
Inside we pulled black curtains
Against the heat and falling bombs
Of sunlight and friends...

3.
No. There was no other way, no other ending...
It was late morning
It was the end of summer
We hugged so hard
We put our lives in a coma—
And left, in separate cars

A Few Lucky Things

The way frost
Leaves a note
On a window in winter

The size of the moon
On a day you lost
More than you should

A missed phone call
A line in a poem

Rainfall

1.
Rain doesn't believe in mist or fog
Or countless shades of grey
Rain doesn't care about "meaning"
Or how well something is said
Especially something called "poetry"

2.
A fall
Is a fall
Is a fall
Says rain…

3.
Rain is a see-through thing
That pushes your real voice
Below your mouth
Dragging your words
Down to earth
Where they pool and puddle
And wait for a long stare of sunlight

To return them to air

Only The Silence

I repeat your name
And nothing changes
We reappear to disappear

Words that should never have been said
And the moment where I could have disagreed
Come and go just the same…

But in the forever presence
And forever absence
Of this summoning

We always appear
To be younger and younger
It's just the silence

Only the silence
That seems to age

The Doctor Will Explain Everything

After the colonoscopy
Surgery was scheduled
"Though I can't imagine
When that would be"
We nodded as if we understood

What a shame you said
Only two days ago
After sunset
We strolled through the garden
Put flowers by the birdbath,
And dad spoke softly

(Mom kept his schedule open, in case of emergencies)

To calm her fears,
She went online
For more information
And took some time
For a much-needed vacation

Then with much consideration
He made his decision
He decided to join a gym
To get in shape
He bought more broth

We gathered in a blue-green room
With yellowed brown chairs
Years ago, expectant fathers
Would wait there, wait and
Smoke, wait and smoke

A groggy surgeon said she would begin
As soon as we put on
Plenty of sunscreen
(Whenever I remember,
I smile)

There were instructions:
Whether you like it or not,
You have to go to bed now...
Take this medication for pain
As often as needed

There were revelations:
No matter how many times I try to stop,
I can't give up chocolate...
Sometimes I don't clean
Under the bed

She slammed the door in a huff
We nodded as if we understood

Memory Of My Daughter Talking
To Her Doll About Life And Poetry

Mommy says she needs sleep
Daddy says he needs shock treatment

I think he's going to stick his finger
In that thing in the wall

You need a bath brown baby
But I won't make you wash your hair

Daddy writes poetry
I can write my name and seven words

Timothy Barbara Cat (and)
I Love You (and) Sarah

Something is called dictation
Where you say a poem without a pen

I told mommy this poem

The squirrel ran up the tree
And a poem fell down on me

I have to practice violin now

The Loss Of Loss

Before they're not terrible
So many things are terrible
Before you realize

They were never terrible
Before you see
Just how unterrible
Things really can be

Such loss of anticipated loss is hard to reconcile...

What will give us meaning
What will be our pleasure
What will make us feel whole

When there is no broken thing
No grief to fill with accusations
No anguish to walk alongside us
With angry theories

About the nature of happiness

The Silence Poem

The white sheet of paper
Before the poem

Your lips reading
These words to yourself

All the snow that fell
Past the windows
Of my childhood home

Me somewhere else
Thinking these thoughts

Winter Weekend

Small winter light
Climbs the sheets
To our eyelids

Fog floats
Above night-let
Snow

We float too

Drifting back
To where
We were

Minutes or years ago

And closing
The cracks
Behind us…

It's Saturday

Maybe Sunday

We Wish You A Happy Birthday

We expect you to arrive in a few minutes
We have come to get you out of there
We are sorry for your loss

We hope you like it here
We hope you don't laugh at what we've done with the place
We came a long time ago

We tried to do the right things
We think you can do better

We wish you a happy birthday

We are sorry for your loss

K Sends Me Her Poems

K sends me her poems to love
It is all we have left
Of another kind of love
My lawyer friends
Say it's a dangerous activity
A kind of disorderly conduct
By persisting...
But sometimes
When the distractions
Of the day have signed off
And the night has lost its signal
I have read things
That make me feel
Like we had children
She never told me about
That we loved each other
In ways we wouldn't say
With eyes we wouldn't open...
K sends me her poems
To have and to hold

Like a flashlight

Death Comes In The Kitchen

Death will come in the window
You thought was locked all these years
The one in the kitchen
The one right above the sink

Death will be tired
And hungry and wanting
A sandwich—all that gravity
Works up a good appetite...

Light from the refrigerator
Unspools on linoleum
Like a break in the clouds
Or a temporary shroud

Death leans into the light
Looking for cold cuts
Spongy white breads and mayonnaise
But you're too healthy for any of that...

So the door closes
And the darkness returns
Until death finds where you're sleeping
And drags you to your absence

Complaining of a certain hunger

Like A Vapor In The Head

That's how we became
The best thing
We can be

Together we are anonymous
Apart, we share
Our souls

If there is an afterlife
I'm counting on
Eternal invisibility

Selections from
Eve And Other Acts Of Defiant Gratitude

After Further Review

1.
The ruling that joy is impossible
Is overturned. The player
Was in full possession of it
And never went out of bounds.
Put 50 years back on the clock.

2.
After review, the ruling that
Old school cloak rooms hid
Nothing but coats and
Winter boots is overturned.
Replay ninth grade.

3.
The ruling on the field is that the receiver
Was incapable of holding on to love
When he reached the end zone.
The ruling stands. What an ass.
Game over.

I Never Woke Up

What you want you will dream—
the life of your neighbor parked in your garage
the blossoms of poppies floating up your arm
and into your head

Driving with hands you can't see,
steering with your eyes, turning on green
and finding your mother in the kitchen
waiting to be fed…

That way you look over your shoulder,
your dark glasses, your confidence in
wakefulness—it's a retelling of how easy
wanting is confused with needing

In a dream something needed me
to stop wanting something it would
not name or point to, and I dreamt

I never woke up.

Light Blue Advertising Agency

The pounding in the head
From the night before
And the client meeting before that

The lost count of scotch and sodas
Missing from the song by the Kingston Trio
And found in the frown on a waitress's face

The boasts about showing the best ads
Known to man—but knowing that mankind
Had almost no desire to read or listen

The never forgetting that what we wanted
Could only happen if a certain "they"
Deigned to voice a certain "yes"…

Still, back at the advertising agency
We loved every minute of our
Near-art, pre-post-modern lives

Each morning being a re-creation of ourselves
From the starting point. Each piece
Renewing its part of the energy

Flowing through floors of polymaths
Breathing in the percussed air of
A non-digitized time on earth

And exhaled in the best works of
Our light-blue, carbon-dated lives

Warm Bricks And A Quick Disguise

The word in prose is stone hard. The word in a poem is like a brick that maintains a fiery core that's curing forever. Poem-words are always becoming something else. Prose words are always repeating themselves. Prose goes after meaning like a fugitive task force. It captures everything it sees. It captivates the reader. But poetry is always on the lam, even when hiding in plain sight. Just yesterday, I saw a poem stop, turn its coat inside out, and walk right past a closely following reader. So it goes.

These Small Frames

Images not quite sure
Of focus, subjects
Taunting King Verb

Flashlights casting about in a world of shadows…

The Book says
Flesh follows words:
Neither of us can get here any other way

So here we are, you and I
Reading this and feeling
All crossed out

Then improved
Then disappointed, then deleted…
Flesh follows words:

To do this thing of ours
Is to feel disassembled
Is to want to leave

But we always stay
Until we're pulled all the way through
These small frames

That somehow, sometimes
Border on wonder

Seven Window Poems

1
Try to remember what you see.
Old age removes memories
Before it removes your eyes.

2
The cold rain doesn't hate your hair.
The blizzard doesn't know about
Your doctor's appointment. Look again.

3
As you can see, frames
Help you focus on the middle.
Things you can't see, surround you.

4
Streams of sunlight. Warmth.
Transparency. Still, it's winter.
What an unclear truth February is.

5
A bird saw a way out
But the exit was something else.
It cost the bird its life.

6
What is seen, is believed.
What you recall, is hidden.
Faith is for your eyes only.

7

At night, the outside
Looks in at the illuminated life
You live. I only see the darkness.

Hypoxia

Nothing
Stays put

The water
The planets
The stars
The heart…

What keeps moving
Cannot be accumulated

There is no museum
Of breathing.

What happens here
Is the first draft

Of who we think we are…
Until hypoxia sets in,

And then we slide ourselves,
Like an essay, under an eternal door

And move on…

Rita On Her Day Off With A Book Of Poetry

Rita stared at page one, poem one,
got to the third stanza, looked up and said
"Where's the 'on' button to this thing?"

Maybe it's that idea in the second line,
the one about "bitterness that leaves
a chemical taste in your mouth"

I offered that up to Rita, but since I was in another poem
("Untitled") 17 pages away, she heard me but couldn't see me...

Rita wrestled with that idea
for a minute or so, flipping
it up and down—like a light switch.

She got up and turned off the music
playing in the kitchen and her bedroom.
And she took off her shoes, thinking

the comfort of slippers will crack
open this poem like a coconut and fill me
with fresh sweet coconut milk

She started over. This time it was different.
The book seemed light in her fingers,
Her clothes seemed to loosen around her body

Her breathing shortened to gasps, until:
"Be quiet. Sit still. You will be unborn
to the circumstances at hand."

What clever cleavage, Rita thought.

Still, it's silly to sit here being unborn on my day off
The errands to run, the soup to make...

I'll read more on Sunday

The Distractions

1.
It isn't like finding some obscure
Symbolic meaning, like say a syringe
In a haystack of fax machines

2.
It's more like driving around with hay
In the trunk of your car, and swearing
It came from a farm on the moon

3.
He desires to have his last breath smell like distractions
In a room filled with distractions—
The plan is to pay no attention at all

4.
She desires the same, but differently
Of course—a spiraling arc of pleasure,
The journey to inner space

5.
Desire keeps us guessing, and not in a good way
Not like predicting when a wave will reach
Our toes on a beach, or how long it should snow

6.
The discharge of invention
Inside an appetite for distraction—
Absorption, expansion, separation: The Milky Way

7.
Even without one eye closed
And a fairly good telescope,
We can see where things will end

The Library (Funny Thing)

In the time of our troubles,
when your therapist made us
wear one mitten and one
surgical glove to work,
I began to record your laughter
secretly. In the theater.
When you were on the phone.
Twice while you were sleeping
and once when I said "I love
all the unreturned books
in your mind."

———

Work began in the library at Eden.
It started the day a secret spoken
memo hung in a golden frame was
somehow copied, read and shredded.
Eternity, instantly became a time
clock. Morning meant you always had
somewhere to be. And long soft days
on colorful blankets became coffee
breaks and cold sandwiches
from unlicensed food trucks.

———

After laughter, your mouth
always tasted like chocolate and
lemonade. Kisses produced beautiful
children who really adored us—
even when they rolled on the floor
laughing at our choices in clothes
and vacation destinations.

―――――

The last days were the hardest. The trips
to the store with buckets of coupons.
The hair splitting and invisible dental decay.
The Library filed liens on our jobs,
and past teachers appeared at hearings
with attendance records and incomplete
assignments. When we laughed, we were
shown the door.

―――――

Thing is, we had no beginning
so this is not the end. What you thought
was my spirit, was only a book
with the pages cut out to hide
another book. One you couldn't
return when you were finished
with it. Funny thing. Funny thing.

Closings And Openings

She closes every email with wishes
For "joy and wonder" above her name

Like a note on a gift...

As if my joy was her wish to grant
As if my wondering keeps her up at night

Who's to say out loud what things
We should wish for in our lives?

But there she is, in her open saffron robe
Saying exactly what I mean

Sorrow

Night comes, filling windows
Like cups of dark coffee
You want to drink alone

But sorrow finds your table
And asks to join you—sitting down
Before you can say "no"

Sorrow wants to talk
And you want to remove sorrow
Like a shirt

But you can't pull it over your head. It won't budge.

Sorrow won't shut up.
Sorrow with its infinite sentences of "Remember when…"
Sorrow with its face leaning over the table and whispering

I came here to find you
And I'm not leaving
Until I do

The Early Birds

Robins hear
Frequencies of the invisible
In almost no light

Before dawn
On my lawn

Worms roar
Like freight trains
In their ears

Let's Say

A morning, let's say. A color, let's say amber, pulsing in a corner of somewhere. A voice revolves in ever-widening circles around your head. Let's say it's the voice of Thomas Edison testing his first phonograph. Then a note, handwritten on lilac colored paper slides under your shoe. You read it in the pulsing amber light. It says "Read only what you don't understand." Let's say you know you're somewhere you've never been before. Let's say you know you're never coming back.

The Queen And The Book

The Queen, wearing a smart turquoise outfit, and haute couture turquoise hat, met with a man who wouldn't read. The meeting was official, and took place in the Queen's Palace. The man wore an unbuttoned blue suit coat and a red tie that descended below the belt and zipper of his massive blue suit pants. It was unclear why the Queen was required to attend to the presence of this man in her kingdom. He was notably vulgar. He lied and he played golf. The country he came from overthrew the rule of Kings and Queens. But there he was, in the Queen's Palace, speaking loudly and slapping the Queen on her back. The Court gasped. Then, recovering from his forbidden touching, she gifted the man a rare book, written by a Hero of the Kingdom. The Court gasped again. Louder. Why not an umbrella imprinted with the Queen's image? Why not a tea cup? Or a pencil touched by the Queen? But a book? A book of great value to a man who wouldn't read? Some said it was a mix-up in paperwork at the House of Lords, others feared it was a sign of the Queen's advanced age. But later, after the palace was scrubbed clean and new dinnerware was ordered, it dawned on everyone. It wasn't a gift at all. *It was a clever punishment!* Bells pealed. Lutes luted. And cheers of "God save the Queen!" erupted once again in homes and alehouses throughout the kingdom.

The Way Of Sorrows

The summer sun. July or August. Wind in the maple trees on the tree lawns pushing warmth, like a low fi sound, down the sidewalk and into the field next to my childhood home. An acre of milkweed and hawthorn trees between our house and the neighbor's. Two lots that didn't sell in 1926 when the block was first built. By the fall of 1929, the families of would-be neighbors would never arrive. Gone to look for work in Cleveland, or back to Newark or Italy or Poland. Summer, 1962. A field of milkweed and chicory blossoms feeding monarch butterflies, and three hawthorn trees with their canopies of limbs that you could slide under. Where I would sit, invisible in its dark grotto of thorns like those used to crown the head of Christ. There, in summer, under the hawthorn trees, it was always a Friday in Lent. It was mass before school. It was the Stations Of The Cross at 3 PM, before going home from school. And there, in that grotto, you could touch prayer beads of bark and thorns; and renew your devotions in the cool darkness hidden in a summer day. The smell of earth dying into earth, again and again. The Way Of The Cross. The Way of Sorrows. It was the Sixth Station, "Jesus is scourged and crowned with thorns." Outside, the sun and the wind pushing warmth like low fi sound down the sidewalk in front of my home and the field next to it, and the rest of Lorain, Ohio.

Tempestuous

"Shake it off."
The Tempest, Act I, Scene 2

The major lyric poet before Shakespeare was?…
Thomas Wyatt. I forgot that. Perhaps you did too.
It also says *(here)* that Harvard University was founded
Twenty years after Shakespeare died; adding that
"Wyatt's was the name of a chain of cafeterias
founded in Texas in 1957."

————

Texas doesn't have a town named after Shakespeare.
Surprising, because it does have a town called Marfa,
named after (a) Marfa Ignatievna in Dostoevsky's
The Brothers Karamazov, or (b) Marfa Strogoff, a character
in Jules Verne's novel *Michael Strogoff*. Nobody's sure.

————

In Roman Catholic churches there are marble half-shells
filled with water blessed by a priest, that flank the
entrances to the nave. It's a special kind of cleaning fluid
for your right hand, the one used to make the sign of
the cross. It's not a secret sign anymore.

————

Thomas Wyatt introduced the Petrarchan sonnet
to the English-speaking world. But it took Shakespeare
to write really, really good ones. Oh, and his plays! Big
beautiful stagey poems. Still, it took centuries to get rid
of what became sonnet addictions, The ABBA-ABBA
dos and don'ts. The geegaws of rhyming.

————

Then there's the failed Roman Catholic, John Donne.
Though his mother was related to Thomas More,
he didn't want to die for being a Catholic, like his
brother, who deceased in jail for sheltering a priest.
Donne, who knew his way around a poem, stopped
attending mass, married cleverly, went to jail for doing
so, and wrote anti-Catholic pamphlets.

———

Jesus stopped the storm that frightened the men
on the Sea of Galilee. But no one could calm the Atlantic
tempest in 1609 that engulfed the *Sea Venture*. Its masts
shorn by gales, the ship was torn apart, beaching survivors
on an island of spells and ghosts; of sorcery, incantations,
and other magics: Bermuda.

———

In Roman Catholic churches, bread is tinctured with wine.
The body and blood of Christ is transubstantiated. The living
and the dead are in communion with the risen Christ, and one
another. A thurifer holds a thurible, as a priest puts incense
on coals, making the air fragrant with the sacred.

———

Time, which in itself is invisible, is in the cellar of words.
Down below the floors of consciousness, mixing things up.
Temptation. Temporary. Tempest. The name of a car made
by General Motors, Pontiac Division, between 1960 and 1970.
Then again from 1987 to 1991. Then never again.

———

In the early morning of Friday, October 21, 2016, I awoke
from a dream. In this dream, the phrase "Through the reigns
of heartfelt utopia" kept repeating itself. I got out of bed and

wrote it down. Reigns. Not reins. Or rains. It was exactly
4:30 AM. It was my 64th birthday.

———

Wyatt's cafeterias closed in 2003. General Motors declared
bankruptcy at approximately 8:00 AM on June 1, 2009.
It had $82 billion in assets and $172 billion in debts.
A financial tempest thundered for days and months.
Thousands of workers lost faith in promises and other
things unseen. The Pontiac Division was disemboweled.

———

In 1608, John Donne wrote *Biathanatos*. A long way from
The Holy Sonnets, here the poet (now clergyman), sets out a
heterodox defense of self-homicide, of suicide. It comes
complete with examples: Sampson, Saul, Judas Iscariot,
and Jesus. "This will prick Death's pride," he thought.
"But I will decide when the bell shall toll for me."

———

Shakespeare wanted to retire. He had a great roster
of money-makers but needed one more. So he wrote
The Tempest, his last play. He wanted out of London.
He wanted to spend time with his wife and grandchild
at New Place, the second largest home in Stratford…
And to purchase Blackfriars Gatehouse, which some
say was a safe house for priests and secret masses.

———

On October 21, 2016, my 64th birthday,
Leonard Cohen released his final musical recording:
You Want It Darker. Seventeen days later he died in his sleep.

The following day, on November 8, 2016,
Donald Trump lost the popular vote 62,979,636
to 65,844,610—and became the 45th president.

Optional Notes

William Shakespeare (1564-1616)
The Tempest (most likely written 1610-1611)

Sir Thomas Wyatt (1503-1542) various sonnets

Motto of Harvard University in English, "Truth"

Wyatt's Cafeterias, founded, Dallas, Texas in 1957.
"Cuisine The Soul of Texas (Some Profound Thoughts
On The Cafeteria Life)," Skip Hollandsworth,
D Magazine, January, 1984

Francesco Petrarch (Petrarca) (1304 -1374)

For more on the Roman Catholic dogmas of
transubstantiation and communion, see *Canons of the
Fourth Lateran Council*, 1215. Notably, Canon 1 and
Article 3, "The Sacrament of the Eucharist,"
Catechism of the Catholic Church.

John Donne (1572-1631) *Death Be Not Proud,
No Man is an Island (Meditation XVII, Devotions upon
Emergent Occasions), Biathanatos* (1608) and various

*An Account of the Incidents, from which the Title and Part
of the Story of Shakespeare's Tempest were derived,
and its true date ascertained*, Edmond Malone, 1808

"1964 Pontiac Tempest GTO Tested,"
Car and Driver Magazine, January 1, 1970

GM History in corporation's archive,
first filed May 2, 2009

Leonard Cohen (1934-2016). *You Want It Darker*,
Columbia/Sony Music, released October 21, 2016

*The Mueller Report (Presented With Related Material
By The Washington Post)* Introduction and Analysis
by Reporters Rosalind S. Helderman and Matt Zapotsky,
2019

See signed indenture of mortgage,
William Shakespeare, March 11, 1613
(British Library)

Our New Names

At that restaurant
when you were about
to speak

When the moment
was about to become
the matter between

our new names
of Plaintiff
and Respondent

I saw you again
studying in the library
100 years before

your beautiful mind
unaware of your
beautiful body

your eyes in a book
by an author who
wouldn't like you

because you could
finish his sentences
before he wrote them

which bored you
which made you
look up and smile

at me staring at you

The Obituaried Inventory Of Likes

For Mary of Loudonville, age unknown,
It was golfing in Florida and her nieces

Robert, 52, born in Chicago, but reared in Newark
Enjoyed his dog Robix, and another named Whisper

Lotti, 91, of Fort Worth
Liked Blue Bell Ice Cream
The Mesquite Rodeo, and Gunsmoke

Because the living have no power over death
Because the dead have no say about the after of their life
Most obituaries leave a trail of questions:

What about that love of Nietzsche
That was burned out of Mary
By golf course sunlight?

What do we call the complex system of phenomenology
That Lotti discovered in the bottom of bowls--the one
That made her doubt the nature of ice and sugar?

And wouldn't it be refreshing
To know that Robert preferred to pretend
That Whisper was a woman that led him on a leash

Naked through Newark

In The Dark

I miss talking to you
So I take old conversations
Out of the giant freezer

And listen to our voices
Thawing out in a room
You've never seen

Wooden Desks

You raised your arms
above your head
and touched your fingers
forming an empty circle

"This is the loophole that none shall pass through"

It was larger than the eye of a needle
and smaller than a camel.
Some of us thought you
were referring to
the paperwork
of love

―――

Back at the blackboard,
20 years before, a nun
in a nun's habit drew a circle
in pink chalk

"This is the hypocenter of an earthquake"

We imagined a deep rumble
coming up through the floor
from the school's steam-heat boiler room,
vibrating our pant legs, thighs and skirts
and rocking our wooden desks
with their holes for inkwells
that we didn't understand
and never used.

Years later, after the marriages
and divorces. After we
ratted each other out
behind the two-way mirrors
of parties and family reunions,
I still don't understand
that gesture: I was no lawyer
and you were no ballerina.

_____

Did the nun know?

Lexeme Dream

Joy is everywhere
And suffering is everywhere
But you and I cannot be
Everywhere at once

Here and there. Here. And there.

Do you remember what you said
When wonder moved boxes of anger
Out of the way, and cleaned off tables
Sticky with the past?

Now and then. Now. And then.

If you can hear me, tell me:
Is all this really just a hiccup of joy?
Is light always a complete sentence
Everywhere you walk over there?

My mother died in her sleep. Age 98.

Do you really die at all
If you die like that?
Or do you just wake up
Go to the bathroom
And start a new dream

Forever…

In Line At The UPS Store

In line at the UPS store
Something about something not packed
Something about time not being there
When most needed

———

I read obits in a newspaper
Still made out of paper. Death notices
The old way. Ones that black-ink your fingers
With words of the end of time

———

The line grows. A thrown-open package
Litters the counter and floor. A small face sobs.
A woman steps forward to comfort,
Her eyes, absorbing pain like blue towels

———

Some pass away. Some go home.
One had a last wish: "Please don't vote for Trump!"
Cleveland Plain Dealer, October, 2016

———

Blue towels to small face:
"It's bad, you're right, but it's not the end
of the world. No one died."

———

There will be other boxes
Other containers, ready to ship
There will be oncoming traffic in the passing lane
There will be things you can't see your way around

———

Meantime, there are other reasons to sob
And the line is backing up, and up and up

Lines Written By A Bass Player

You can't see anything if you look with your mouth. So the phone is silenced. I'm in the car, the sun is setting. It's Winter O' Clock. Snow is dusting the road and jumping up and around the tires in front of me. I'm thinking about the road turning colder and colder and wrapped in whiter and whiter sheets. I'm thinking about driving on a tiny corner of the earth's winding sheet. I'm thinking about gravity's great love for us all. Keeping us from flying off the round edges of the world. Keeping us grounded. I'm thinking how maybe gravity loves too much; forcing us to build bigger and bigger rockets to get away. To take a break somewhere gravity can't reach us. But today, like every day about now, I'm heading home from the gym to feed the cat and maybe make my wife laugh. Later I'll write a poem about the simple, tiny, perfect lines a bass player wrote and played in a famous song. Amazing. It's like a poem within a poem. I hope I can pull it off.

Upbeat Emails From The Poem Family

The poem doesn't mean to scare you. It just calls in the middle of the night because it knows that's when you'll be home. Unlike novels, a poem can blend in perfectly with the work papers on your desk, the work you're avoiding—the work they pay you for. That poem you lost when your car ran out of gas on the coldest night in Oklahoma history? It never held it against you. Stop fretting. Finally, as a book, poems know the other books will laugh at them. It doesn't care. You don't have to hide it by a bookend. Talk to you soon.

Dark Matter (II)

Some say the heart of the universe is a black hole. Dark matter at the edge of time and eternity. A ferocious nothingness, sucking everything and everyone into forever absence. But at the center of our little affection (I've tried to say this before) was nothing but a cup of black coffee. That, and my need to talk about the structure of Jobim's *Trem Azul*, and Portuguese verbs. It was never lives of happiness at the edge of darkness. It was always coffee, near the brim of a cup, made with water from the River of Saudade.

The Desired

The cake, the soufflé, the salmon.
The yellow dress, the antique bed, the view of Paris.
The lanky tour guide, the small museum, the translator
Studying for her medical license.
The croissants with jelly, the five photos
Taken by three women and two men.
The departure from the hotel
The flight home, the shower
We shared before unpacking.
As usual, it's only desire
That leaves so much
To be desired.

The End Of The Movement

The traffic slowed then stopped.
The cars and trucks froze as if
on a screen. No one could be
added or deleted. The program
for getting home would not respond.

—

You slowed, then stopped for
a photo I still have. You're
squinting at something we can
not see, your hand to your ear
as if you can't hear me, or
you're listening to years that
we haven't lived yet.

—

My mother's heart slowed then stopped.
Her blood's great work, was finished.
The light in her eyes flickered,
then fixed on the ceiling, as
the doors to her heart closed.

—

On the wall, a still life someone's father
brought home from the last French
gallery left in Da Nang. A half-loaf of
bread by a cracked vase with yellow
snapdragons. A thick lacquer applied
to keep the colors in place.

Different Meanings

The stagecoach arrived late.
Dusty from elsewhere. The actors
Mused where that was. Then
Began to rehearse.

Some say argument discovers truth.
Others say it buries truth the way
A photograph buries a painting
Of a photograph.

Each day I drive by a Day Care Center.
You know what they look like: plastic
Things in primary colors; children
Without a care in the world.

A farmer in a huge machine is laughing.
He waves at us as we stare. Bales of
Hay flopping in another large machine.
Later, horses consume his joy.

In England, five women wore large
hats at a play we finally got tickets to.
I whispered to one, "The hats. Really?"
"I don't take your meaning," she said.

The Lines Of Your Thinking

We followed the lines of your thinking,
And reached a snowy mountaintop.

We stepped over the remains of those who got there first
And found you drinking heavily in a sprawling shack of books.

We were hungry, and you did not feed us.
We were thirsty, and you did not offer us water.
We were cold, and you said "Hey, things happen…"

You gave us a box of books we had already read
And said, "Burn these for warmth
Then show yourselves out."

The Permissions Company

*Permissions research and negotiation can make you
want to tear your hair out.*
The Permissions Company, Inc.

The line formed early and lasted
Until the doors were locked for the day
Some had faces on the verge of turning
Into clouds, others had hands disfigured
By years of prayerful supplication
Some had knees turned to mush
From decades of obeisance

Some carried empty bags,
Others, photos of people
They wanted to love
Some carried books filled
With things they wanted to say

Inside, some saw their mother, some
Their father, with a strange look on
Their face; in a conference room
Some saw former teachers and bosses
Seated at tiny desks, staring at a
Blackboard where it was written
Always ask for permission first

They had that same look

Seven Moon Poems

1

On a warm night the wind will
push lake breeze through
the windows of an empty car.
The moon will see things differently.

2

There's the life we live,
the life we want, and the life
we will regret. The moon takes
notes. The moon keeps count.

3

The moon witnesses crimes
the sun will never see. It speaks
every dialect of fear, knows
and numbers every dark urge.

4

Summer. Waves touch the sand
of a public beach. Summer wind
cuts through layers of body heat.
The moon glowers at hidden figures.

5

We worship the sun, but welcome the moon.
One says "soon," the other says "now!"
One radiates. The other insinuates.
One looks down. The other looks around.

6

The moon is the nosiest neighbor
you will ever have. Keep your wits
about you. There's no such thing
as a moonless night. Close the blinds.

7

Some say the moon was struck and
half-blinded by cosmic debris. Perhaps so.
But the moon can hear better than
the sun. That's why we turn on music.

That's why we whisper.

When You Didn't Respond

When you didn't respond to my
thoughtful emails, I received a batch
you didn't know you had sent. A sadness
with the same address as yours
was there, every time I checked.

———

Your voice once changed my life.
It was air that let me swim to the surface.
To sunlight and more air. Air to say thank you
for your perpetual joy.

———

Then time and thoughts changed your breathing.
Boredom shortened your sentences. I became
someone who made the mistake of wanting
to be loved out loud—the usual flaw
of putting desire into nearby words.

———

If I know what you will not say, who then is speaking?
If we both know what we won't say out loud,
are we still speaking? I only ask, because your voice
once changed my life. But nothing like this silence.

Please Don't Hum

Please don't hum
Or tell me about another poem
That's "really great" while reading this

Don't visualize me on the other side of this paper

Standing in my kitchen
Hearing the cat crunch his food in the corner
While you read out loud

Please, just this once,
Let us quietly fall in love forever
With the same person

Questionnaire

If a poem falls off my desk, and is trampled on
By the cat, and scuffed by the bottom of the baby's diaper,

And sticks to the shoe of a policeman,
And tumbles a block in the wind,

Where it's sucked through the front door

Of the company you work for
As the cleaning crew leaves at midnight,

And is picked up by the night security guard
Who puts it in the break room by the doughnuts,

Where someone who thinks you like
"that kind of stuff" puts it on your desk

And you wad it up, unread, and throw it
Into a wastepaper basket,

Is it still a poem?
I don't know...

If you go to work and do
Just about nothing day after day

But still get paid, year after year,
Did you really go to work?

Poem On Writing Poems

If you say you are writing
just for yourself, call everything
a beginning. It doesn't matter where
the ending takes you. But know
it will always get there ahead of you.

"Not ideas, but things." Yes. But things
doing things they weren't supposed
to do, is a better idea. Let the wheelbarrow
do a rain dance. Have a plum eat a poem.
Be the best hyphenated-poet you can be. (1)

What you remember
is the oldest and brightest blood
within you. When it comes
around, let it fill your heart
to the brim.

When nobody tells you
what your style is, thank them.
When no one says your work
reminds them of so and so
know you are free. Get busy.

Don't imitate the famous names. They were
as sure as you that their poems were (or
will be) a fraud. Borrowing their voice
will only make you cough, and your
poems will look like half-eaten pastry.

Don't write poems to be read
after you're dead. Write poems to your

16-year-old self. Let her know how well
things worked out. Tell him
he was right. Enjoy the endings.

I know they pounded "Make it new"
into you. I know you are tired of carrying
that leather bag through empty, dusty
train stations. Don't. The saying wasn't
even new, it was Confucius. Make it up. (2)

If you expect someone to listen to your
poem, imagine more than their eyes and
ears. Respect the gift of their time, and
imagine the bad days they have endured.
It will help you get somewhere together.

For centuries, popular songs have had
an average length of two minutes and
twenty-six seconds. You can look that
up and listen for days. Start anywhere,
but start. Write to the poem's 2:26

Eve was stronger than Adam.
And braver. Eve wanted to know
what's what. Adam watched creation
and named animals. Eve found out
what creation tastes like. Be Eve. (3)

Optional Notes

(1) William Carlos Williams, "A Sort of Song" Poetry Magazine,
1914 and *Patterson Book I* (1927), "The Red Wheelbarrow" and

"This Is Just To Say," in The Collected Poems of William Carlos Williams, Volume I (1938)

(2) *Make It New Essays*, Ezra Pound, (Faber & Faber), London, 1934, "In a Station of the Metro," Poetry Magazine, (1913)

(3) *Book of Genesis*, Chapter 3

Discernment

In the morning I lay out versions of myself.
I put them on the bed, and drape them
over a chair. I pace back and forth, or
I sit on the floor drinking tea
and staring at the choices.

Sometimes it's hard to separate a prayer
from a wish, a belief from the weariness
of asking more questions. Mornings can
break your resolve. You say "where do
I sign?" But a poem says "don't you dare!"

I live on the shore of a Great Lake.
41.4993° N, 81.6944° W. On the other shore,
42 miles due north, everything is the same.
Even Daylight Savings Time. It's hard to see,
but that's me waving to me from Canada.

At the autopsy of the star, the gallery
was filled with eager listeners. "A collision
with ideas, is noted. There's some concept
scarring. But a constant loss of light
through wormholes was the cause of death."

In the morning I separate the night
from my other thoughts. It's like laundry.
I don't want the darkness to bleed through
the brightness. But it happens. So I'm off
to work like that—hoping no one notices.

Desire Never Gets A Snow Day

Desire never gets a snow day.
It bundles you up
And shovels the driveway.

Even warms up the car for you.

—

In eighth grade I whispered to the girl
Seated in front of me: "What did the telephone
Operator say to the fisherman?" She shrugged.

"I have salmon on the line."

—

Outside the ER doors
The voices of smokers
Push through a grey cloud of tobacco.

Inside, people are waiting to tell them something.

—

A man (near your age) reads his emails harshly.
He wants something he doesn't see there.
He worries it's not a mistake, or an oversight.

He feels foolish. But keeps reading.

—

If happiness is a cheering crowd,
Then desire is the empty seat belonging
To someone still driving around outside

Looking for a place to park.

The Book Of Revelation: *An Introduction*

Excerpts from this long poem appeared previously in *Road, Frame, Window* (parts X and XI) and in *Invisible* (part XII).

This marks the first appearance of the poem in its entirety. It was completed in March, 1990.

The Book Of Revelation

Most find their answer
in the Holy Bible
next to Genesis
or the page after
the Book of Revelation
I found mine
In *The History of Religious Orders*
By the Rev. Charles Warren Currier,
(A Compendious And Popular Sketch
of the Rise And Progress of The Principal
Monastic, Canonical, Military, Mendicant
And Clerical Orders) Boston,
MacConnell Brothers & Co., 1896 ...
Timothy Donohue, December 15, 1847
Married Rose Lackey
September 9, 1873
Daniel P. Donohue, July 13, 1874
John P. Donohue, April 20, 1876
Timothy Donohue, March 30, 1878
Kittie Donohue, December 12, 1880
Mary Donohue, March 7, 1886
Lillie Donohue, July 4, 1889
Rosetta Donohue, October 12, 1897
John P. Donohue (468 Milford
Street, Cleveland) married
Jane Ellen Cummings, June 7, 1901
Lucille Donohue, July 21, 1903
Gertrude Donohue, 1905
Timothy Edmund Donohue, 1907 ...

I.
14 years, one wife, one child and one divorce later
I returned to Ohio

And found the missing limbs
of the family tree
in a history of celibacy
stuffed under socks
of virgin wool
made to cover the stumps
of amputees---there
in faded purple ink
dissolving in late October sunlight
bold-stroked and serifed
was the missing loiny litany
my name in the handwritten history
of my grandfather---the record
kept in a book whose contents
made it seem
as if we were all the punchline
of a drunken Irish Joke
that's passed on
from generation
to generation …

II.
The railroad of the father
amputated the leg of the son
two days before he was to marry the girl
… it amputated the leg
and everyone
paid and paid and paid

drunk
he fell
into his 82nd year---
but he held on
to all of us, so …
in time,
we all got
smashed …
if he does walk again
he'll limp to his grave
with a new limb
the hole and stone
are bought
and when the weather breaks
I'll trim back the weeds
as he requested
you'll miss me when I'm gone
you'll miss me when I'm gone
you'll miss me when I'm gone
he said so
all our lives
when I was young
I knew it as a sad prediction
now I know it's a sad and hopeful
request---I'll put you in the book I say
you'll be recorded---he smiles
he thinks I mean a novel
he thinks I'm going to bring out
a tape recorder
he thinks I'm my brother Ed
in the morning
my brother Dave
in the afternoon
my brother Paul

off again to Africa
at night---Why don't you ever say
you miss your own father?
Why did you tell me how I'd feel when you died---
then go on and on living---What?
Too deaf, rarely is it too bad about what's missed
and rarely do I repeat
the screaming-feeling
truth---I'LL PUT YOU IN THE BOOK I SAID!
Oh. It better be A GOOD BOOK!
It's not---I whisper

III.

> "Language can do what it can't say."
> -William Stafford
> Oberlin College, November 13, 1989

I have been trying to get over
that first word
to jumpstart somewhere else
to bust an artery in a conversation
with an old stone house
where the bones call
long distance---to connect
with anything other than how
this lazy personal pronoun
thinks or feels---
"Just look out the window
and ask the lady to dance"
says the older, richer poet
And when I do: I hear a bird
asleep on a humming wire

and my daughter humming to herself
alone in her bedroom in Texas
and the spokes of a bicycle wheel
twisting in north
northwest wind
I look out the window
remembering a day now
ten years and twelve hundred miles
away, when the first and only word
she knew
and said
was "Daddy"

Dad, I'm the stone
next to yours
and I've made your oldest son
promise me it will say
"At least I'm not in Texas"
as an invitation to dance on our graves, to look at us
laying there side by side
and have a laugh

From this distance
I don't know what my daughter sees
in me---but whatever it is,
unlike you, I won't tell her
how to feel

when it goes

Until then,
look out this window
and repeat after me:

"Come on baby,
let's do the twist

Oh come on baby
let's do the twist"

IV.
The farmer to the south has erected a bright orange
snow fence to protect the entry to his root cellar
and interrupt the path of deer hunters on his land.
This blood-money land awarded Revolutionary War
soldiers called eerie by settlers and "land of the large
river" by the Chippewa and Iroquois. It is a land of
lilac and iris, snapdragon, peony, daffodil and jack-in-
the-pulpit. Woods thickened by scotch-pine, blue-fir
and hawthorn trees rise everywhere south of the
steel-hard and ship-yarded cities of Cleveland and
Lorain, where the soil shifts to the sand shore of
the lake. North of there: Canada. South: a grid of
farms cut in forests of silver and Canadian maple,
sycamore and Dutch elm as far as any eye on glacier-
flattened land can see.

V.
Without a thought of staying
I went west to Texas
and lacking the same
thought I returned
to Ohio—
I teach courses

in "expository
writing" at the local college
a hopeless task anywhere
here I call the roll
and it seems like
I'm being handed
an obituary for
everyone who died
while I was gone
names I thought
I'd never hear again
I pronounce easily:
Serbian, Italian,
Ukrainian, Romanian,
Irish, Czech, Polish
Slovenian and Puerto Rican
Sons and grandsons
of shipbuilders
and autoworkers
the daughters
and grandchildren
of steelworkers
railroad men
bakers
and butchers:

Svete
Stacho
Stitak
Catalano
Konya
McDougal
Seca ...

I know them/don't know them/all
I hear their "dems" and "dese"
and "got no" in the hall
I read their essays
written in the casual-authoritative tone
of a backhoe operator
talking to the guy
in the ditch
or their father
come home omnipotently drunk
after the union voted
a walkout

And I want to give them all "A's"

"A" for not leaving their fathers and mothers
and this farm-rich but business broken land,
for getting drunk at the big Polock wedding
and kneeling to pray the next day---
for being the Orthodox Rite of the American dream

They go to the weddings
They bury the dead
They sit in the white-glare
Of the local college classroom
To "better myself"

And sometimes, between the last grade
on the last paper and the falling asleep
I think: they have. They have made me "better."

And somehow, when I say their names slowly
I think the simple fact that they and their families
are still here becomes an act of holiness…

Something you write within,
Never "about"

VI.
It was one of the worst fractures I've ever seen
said the doctor with the nose of a ship's surgeon.
Imagine raising a piece of porcelain, a cup say,
above your head and hurling it down on the floor.
The way I see it, as he was falling he tried to
shift the weight into the artificial leg, that
snapped the thigh, but the bone was held as if
it was in a vise in the prosthesis. So, when he
hit, it all shattered. Had to. He pushes an
X-ray across his desk like a dustpan: see for
yourself. When he mentions the part about being
drunk, I take mother out of the room. But I don't
return with a broom.

VII.
At the corner of the Shell station
and the art museum in Oberlin, Ohio
I hear voices

I'm talking to a hitchhiker
I picked up at this corner
Twenty years before

Yes I'm going to Lorain
But nothing came out of his mouth
After that question

He made conversation
through the pulpy white mounds
and half-healed red scales
of the razor-bled wrists
at the end of the green
fatigue jacket

And Betty today
talking talking talking
about why we went to this meeting
to talk about our fathers and mothers:

I know one thing: you're not ready for this
This was a bad idea. I've got to get back to Lorain
Do you have any idea where you're at?

Three students cross under the light at an angle
Arms linked together
Rain rolling off the backs
Of their long black coats

It would have worked
If I'd gone up the veins
In the movies, they always go across

You minimize everything that went on
In Texas, in Chicago,
In your life
I don't think
You've been honest
With me---I'm confused
How should I maximize it Betty?
Every word you speak to me
Comes out wrapped in bolts

Of hospital gauze

But I don't stand in your bloody pools
Of rage and blame
And I cannot unsleep your dead father
To hear how you have healed yourself
Of him

What is that perfume you are wearing?
It's called "Listen"
I stole it from my daughter---
Then an exaggerated almost imaginary silence

As a wet silver razor headed due north
And twenty years
Forward
And backwards

Yes Betty, I have a good idea where we're at
This isn't Texas
Anymore

VIII.
--- a month in traction, two in a rest home.
Daily visits bringing the mail, the newspapers
the get-well-soon and Christmas cards. The bone
unbelievably healed, but an ever-lengthening list
of new complaints and a new plastic rosary; each
decade, another of the primary colors. He has lived
through every one this century offered. Son-husband-
father of four boys. We knew the foot he threatened to
put down was a phony one. "You boys don't know what

115

it's like to live with a leg off; to be a cripple".
Who am I to say that his tenacious hold on an artificial
limb didn't save him when he jumped out of life.
That he buried the real leg he was meant to stand on.
We hope you're right dad. We hope we still don't know.
But most of all, here with you in this house of
sleep and death, I hope you're forgetting.

IX.   "Green winter; full graveyard"
                                                --Midwest folk saying

She read Hesse
Maslow
Dostoevsky
Chardin---was
A homecoming
Queen
Whose court divorced her
Eighteen years later
Whose every failure
Is boiled down
To the literal
"Likely story":
Being here
Being alive
Being unsuccessful
In drinking
Only her
And only
With my
Eyes ... Or
The con-
Vulsions

That ended
My drinking
To death
Attempt---It doesn't matter
How you paginate the days
Of the years zero to eighteen
It's the story
Our daughter reads
Into the text
That matters
Even if I glue
Half of page one
To page 100
And the middle
Starts with
"Once upon a time"
And the part
Where you didn't stay
And didn't die
Doesn't say
Happy
Or for-
Ever …

She read Hesse, Maslow, Dostoevsky …

Didn't we all?

X.
On the day we brought him home, after I'd carried his
television, a few clothes in a plastic bag and his
shaving and denture kits to the car; after I'd wheeled

him to the front desk where mother signed papers, each
with the heading "Party of Responsibility" I went
to the dining room and joined two nurses having a
smoke. A woman I had seen many times, whose room was
across the hall from my father's rolled to a stop
at my chair, pointed to a spot on the floor near my
feet and said "Is that your child?" I looked at the
spot. "No," I said. And still pointing at this small
red spot on the carpet she spoke to the nurses. "He
says that isn't his child, but he doesn't see the child.
It's too much of an illusion for him."

XI.
Full moon
hard freeze
the sound of feet
breaking the bones of snow

Above me
the old sentence sleeps
in baggy blue pajamas
in an antique leather chair
by a moonlit window

I can tell you that I know
the only thing this old sentence
dreams about is
ears! ears! ears!

But thinking of it
small and curled in moonlight
I have no urge

and no reason
to prove it

A cigarette glows
at the tip of my face
the moon above us all---

Something connects the dots
something connects me with
an invisible hyphen
from within to without
from here to everywhere
and I sense the presence
of something that punctuates
my life with kindness---

It's not something in this land
but of it, and of the moon above it
and through all the sentences below it

XII.
A jagged line of trees breaks cooperatively at the
window of the den. From the bird feeder in the foreground,
the picture deepens and lengthens; the grass and the
farmer's field deep with snow, and the morning sky
soft soiled bolts of Irish linen: more on the way.
Colored statues come to life. Unposed jays and native
cardinals peck at opposite sides of the free breakfast.
It's hard to be proud when you're hungry; and every
winter here is a hard one. "When I put something out
of my mind, I subtract a lot of details," says mother
trying to answer one of my questions. And I think

how our lives are most real when we focus on the details
we have given it---just like a work of prose fiction
gets "real" in direct relation to the amount of sen-
sory specifications---details---the author has written
into the book. Leaving me to wonder what fiction it was
that my mother "forgot." And which ones I'm trying/
not trying to.

—March, 1990
Avon, Ohio

Crippled By The Clouds

An Afterword to
The Book Of Revelation

The poem, Crippled By The Clouds, revisits some of the same subject matter covered in The Book Of Revelation, more than three decades later. It was completed in January, 2022.

It serves here as a kind of Afterword to The Book Of Revelation.

Crippled By The Clouds

I carry my father's
severed leg with me. I lost it once,
but someone screamed
and I hurried back
and found it.

———

*"You don't know what
it's like to be a cripple"*
my father said. He said
it again about a week later.
Then, nearly every day.

———

"You don't know…" was a phrase in the air
like a cold front moving through our house;
the words turning to fog and clouds
that filled every room.

———

What I understand is this:
what's severed can itch;
can stub its invisible toe,
and get leg cramps from
legless running.

———

On the day I left for college,

four miles down the road
I turned around and woke up

my dad to say: "I didn't
forget it; well I did, but I
got it now."

———

Although it was severed
in August of 1937, this leg is
always as new as the day it
dropped next to rail tracks.
It's always exactly 29 years
10 months and 12 days old.

———

Once I was going to hand the limb
back to my father to keep until
he told me what he wanted me
to do with it. But I already knew:
he wanted exactly what I was doing.

———

There's no real conclusion
between me and my father's leg.
What's gone remains. But what
remains isn't always so true—
like the word "know"
or the arc of this poem.

––––––

Meantime I wait for a real hand to
reach through dreamed sunshine
and take us all away. I know it's out
there, but not anywhere I can see.
Maybe it's been severed by glare.
Maybe it's crippled by clouds.

—January, 2022
Rocky River, Ohio

NEW POEMS

As Close As I Can Get

You say what I know
but have forgotten.

Say, how I was shoveling snow,
how you were watching from the window.

You detail what it was like:
the wet gloves, the drifts reforming wind by wind…

Hours later, I ask you to tell me again
and it starts all over:

You speaking, me listening
 as close as I can,

to the life I live
inside you.

Warm And Alone

"None of us has long, we hear, and just so many poems left."
- David Young, *Phenomenology for Dummies*

The coffee cools.
The poem comes.
The poem goes.

A friend told me
he saw his poem
roll down the side
of a snowy mountain.

My poem wasn't
that far up. But
it got windy, so

it found a bench
on the shady side
of a sunlit hill

where it waited
for me to catch up.
I listened for its cough.

When I arrived,
my breath was sour
and the poem was gone.
On the bench was a
warm spot where it had sat,
and I sat there too.

Knowing *this*,
will be as close
as I can get.

Still, When This Table Is Empty

—Thanksgiving with Dan and Virginia

Still, when this table
is empty, when winter
whites the windows,
and spring redraws
its curtains, when a
hundred fires have
come and gone on
summer beaches,
a part of me will
return to this chair
and remember you
all—and be grateful,
still and again.

Some See Something

Some see something
And write a love letter
Others keep looking

For two cups of water
Hidden under a moonless desert
Or a two-car accident on a quiet driveway

Some see a pornography
Of thirst and silence
In letters with no return address

That Flushed Poem Hidden In Your Face

That flushed poem hidden in your face
is wider than the poem you carry
in your breath. And the poem

you carry in your feet is grateful
for those shoes you wear in winter
and the flip flops of summer. But Oh,

those green poems that look up to you
like a field of clover. They're just hoping
to get rid of you, step by step. That said,

we could go on naming the body parts
anyone can find hidden in any poem,
but that's not the point. The point

is that the poem you get at birth
isn't the one you'll decease with. Something
to remember while shoeing over the dead.

Gate Assignments

You won't find in the clouds
that which you left behind
in your rush to the airport.

Nothing of your panic to lift
yourself up from all that's been
dragging you down.

Relax. Your fears can't
fit under the seat
in front of you—

can't be bent into
the compartments
above your head.

Read from your book.
Offer your unopened bags
of peanuts to someone

sitting near you. Your drinks
to another. Read. Then wait for
the plane to come to a full stop...

Where you'll be asked
to listen closely, as gates
for connecting flights

may have changed.

The Clouds Are Drinking Coffee

Clouds in a blue sky
are drinking coffee
we can't taste,

and jumping around
something we can't see...

The sky is opening
its giant blue lips
and gulping down the clouds.

We look up with our cups.

The Book Of Us On Vacation

The book opened up for us,
welcomed us, hugged and squeezed
our spines.

———

Later, the book arrested us,
warned us to slow down.
Reminded us, we were
on vacation.

———

Then, three nights in a row,
the book poked us in our sleep
saying "Put some coffee on.
Something's not right."

———

That was the end of us.

The Man In The Waiting Room

Like a dog that wants the future
To remember where he was

The man in the waiting room
Reads his book with a yellow Highlighter

Sniffing out the past, and making
His own mark on the created world

Taking Shape

All thoughts are born round
and waiting to talk back;
to grow longer legs and run
down a road you can't see.

———

When a thought is sharpened,
what's been chipped away is
saved in green felt pouches
and delivered to dictionaries.

———

A round thought is always
shaped by the place it was
born—something you may
or may not have seen in
a photograph or novel.

———

You can buy a round thought
like a round of drinks—your belly
pushing into a popular bar. Later,
things will blur, your thinking
will have no edges again.

———

A millstone is a round thought
with an absence in the middle; a hole
that lets you grind other thoughts
down to sizes you can carry with you.

———

What comes out round, usually goes astray.
The fads. The infections. The mistakes.
Some walk to the edge of a sentence
and jump off—only to come back round.

An Englishman In The Barbequeue

An Englishman, curious at the number of insulting and catty comments he heard while waiting in line to be seated at a recommended restaurant, deduced that the term "barbecue" was an Americanism used to describe individuals lined up to disparage one another prior to enjoying a meal. Fascinated, he left a message at his office in London, "Hungry, but enjoying what they call barbequeue. The Yanks are no match for an Eton man! Home on Wednesday."

One Day In A Library
In Steubenville, Ohio

A moist wind blew through
the library, pushing August humidity
through the stacks. The air sweet

with that cryptic smell of a new
baby's head, and tinged with notes
of leather and aging paper. That's where

you appeared, your brain magnifying
footnotes, to absorb the last learned
particles of an academic article,

and sourcing the adumbrations of
an author's assumptions, and
degrees of pedagogy. I was just

a witness. One with a numbed
tongue, like I'd been drinking
doubles of novocaine.

And here I am 50 years later
still struggling to say a word.

Sunyata

Like a front desk clerk
you showed me
all your emptinesses.

I picked one,
left my clothes in the car,
and locked the door twice

from inside.

Sandwich

The sandwich
had enough of us,
and left.

Now, you and I
are just two people
alone. Trying

to find the bottom
of this page; the last
bite of a poem

we can't quite digest.

Ordering, Dining, Conversing

And what can we get for you tonight?

I will have greens with umbrage
followed by umbos of mushroom. Also,
I will shout at the waiter inside of me.

Excellent choices. And for you?

I will have pieces of burnt umber toast
followed by your best umbles pie. Also,
I will scream into squalid napkins.

Very good then!

The Well Vacuumed Word

Sometimes you have to take a vacuum cleaner to a word and suck up the dust and debris hiding all the other lives it has had. All the births. All the deaths. All the resurrections and insurrections it has participated in.

All a word ever needs is to be uncovered by a new crop of human atoms.

Bodies Of Water

Perhaps because we emerged
from prehistoric salt oceans,
perhaps because the world
is more water than land,
we speak of *bodies*

of water.

––––––

Water covers
71% of the planet.
Our hearts and brains
are 73% water; the lungs
83%. Skin is 64% water.
Even our bones
are 31% water.

––––––

No one can drink
the oceans of their birth.
It's nature's way of saying
you can't go back home.
It's why all our memories
are searching for water.

––––––

It's why we fear dying
thirsty, and alone.

Subtrahends

In the possession
Of every remainder

Is a photo album

Of what love
Minus forgiveness
Looks like

Looks like

Jars Of Fog: Reading Caroline Gordon

> "Every life is a defense of a particular form."
> —Anton Webern

She wrote in a way
I couldn't see my way through.

A soup of Southern dialect,
lost causes, Gothic insanity

and Catholic symbolism.
Each story, every novel

a new jar of fog
with an airtight lid.

A Farewell

In memory of Caroline Gordon Tate (1895-1981)

The end of the prescient nescient
become an intractable
predictable believer.

I expected a face
growling on a pillow,
skin lineated by gin,
eyes burned out
by neglected novels.

I was right.
I was wrong.
I was there.

Hart Crane

See *The Broken Tower (A Life Of Hart Crane)*
by Paul Mariani (1999) p. 94

There in a dentist's chair
in quotidian Cleveland,
amid the world of
ad writing and snow
and boredom, he
had touched on
the world of infinite
consanguinities.

And as the drill
bored into his tooth,
he followed its every spiral,
as if he were already dead
and watching a body—
his body?—at a funeral.

Rain

Rain.
Three days
Straight.

Things wash away...

Already
I have said
Too much.

Late August To Late September

Sun on sand and water. Beige-browns and blue-greens.
Somewhere someone is heading to a beach to go swimming.
Somewhere someone is heading to a beach to stop swimming.
One gooey with joy, one cracked by fears of drowning.

———

A couple reading printed things. Big beach towels and books
held between the sun and their faces. They sense words floating
in the personal eclipses they have made. The shadows warn them
something is coming and not going away.

———

Eventually, summer turns its back on everyone. Leaves
leave colored notes in trees. Reds and yellow-greens.
Still the swimmers and readers come and go. Some gasping
and grateful to be back on land. Others just diving in.

Night List

I

I make a list at night of things
for tomorrow. A book to finish,
a song to listen to, a friend to call,
a resentment to let go of. Knowing
that only the scratches on paper
are guaranteed to be present
in the morning.

II

I received a letter providing proof
you've given up on great books.
Your thralldom with 1950's tv reruns
is startling. Where do you put
all the memories of how we once
lived only for art and lust?

III

Maybe it was the 80's. Maybe it was
me and my belief in how we could
squeeze so many lives into our veins.
I remember laughter. The welcome
darkness of that big city. Drapes drawn
on the blinding lights of jobs and distance.

IV

In the trick we played on ourselves,
we believed that our theorem of two minus
one equals two, would never be disproved.
But it was. And we ended hard.
I ended hard.

V

I wrote someone else's name
on the back of the photo you sent.
I changed the date too. That way, should
something happen to me in the night,
neither of us will be here in the morning.

Every Now And Then

Every now and then
Reality gets bored with me
And leaves. I don't know
Where it goes, or what it does.

Smoke a cigarette—despite the dangers?
Jog around the park?
Eat a pizza under a tree? I don't know.
But I enjoy its absence.

Then my thoughts are indisputable.
Then my choices are perfect.
My mouth fills with the sweetness
Of cherry tomatoes and dried mangoes. My head

Fills with the scent of freshly brewed coffee
That I drink cup after cup—without walking
Into a kitchen, or washing a cup. But best of all,
Every now and then,

I feel there's something inside of me
That will live forever.

The Last Word On Words

Where did you
put my hope
in the impossible?

I put it by your keys
on the bookcase.

Where did you
put my suffering God
in the suffering world?

I put it in that
picture of Jesus,
hanging in the hallway.

I am through
with your ideas
on ideas—

through with you
having the last word
on words.

Where did you
put my silence?

I put it by a window
that can't be opened.

Cafe, Summer Of '68

Summer delivers
an unsigned postcard:

"Some are here
and some are gone."

I want more words.

———

Two blue-haired
twenty-somethings

cut in front of me.

"No need for a menu,"
says the boy.

"We always know what we want,"
says the girl.

———

A waitress, appearing
to be near my age,

comes with a menu.
I thank her.

But she already knows
what I want. I want everything

that couple is having.

———

Summer delivers
an unsigned postcard:

"Some are here
and some are gone."

I want more words.

I want more time.

One Hundred Syllables
Divided By Ten Things

On The Mind
Furnish daily.

_____

Some assembly
required.

On Loss
My thoughts
are always
with you.

_____

Give
them
back.

On Longing
You misread
the invitation.

_____

I left.

On Doughnuts
Life gets punctured.
Pull over.

_____

Get
doughnut.

On Vowels
Draught for drought-
one vowel

_____

quenches
your thirst.

On John Donne's Betrothal
What could
Anne More say

_____

but "John,
I'm Donne now."

On One Thing After Another
Something
is always

_____

not going
to be.

On Amicable Divorcements
Not an ounce
of truth.

_____

But not
one harsh
word.

On The Defense Of Zen
Don't say anything.

_____

Deny everything.

On Rewriting
Put the poem
down.

_____

Sniff fingers.
Repeat.

Every Before Is Again

They were invisible things
living mouth-to-mouth
in the visible world.

––––––

They were armies
that assembled to attack armies
on empty plains of oxygen.

––––––

Then speech grew
body parts.

––––––

Then symbols were cut in clay
and sunk in papyrus.

––––––

Then the lions.
Then the birdcalls.

––––––

Then you.

––––––

Now, every before is again.
Every then, is a now.

Things Know

Things know things…

———

This half-lit room
This hospital bed
This green chair

———

A green wave knows
it will go back. A green
leaf knows it can't stay.

———

Things know…

———

We do too.

The Dream Window

In a dream, a patient is left
in a dream—banging
on a window through which
he sees himself staring at himself
banging on a window—
in a dream.

He sees himself waking up.
He sees himself writing a note.
Then someone he can't see
says, "Goodbye.
It's time now."
He repeats the phrase
but has no voice.

The patient hears his fists
banging on a window.
A car stops across the street,
and he sees himself look away from himself…
as that person gets in the car,
and it drives away.

The patient hears a car idling in his garage.
The patient hears his garage door coming down.
"Winter windows frost over in silence—until they crack."
He repeats "Winter windows frost-over in silence…"
but has no voice.

In a dream, a patient is left
in a dream—-banging
on a window through which
he sees himself staring at himself
banging on a window—
in a dream.

The Dream Museum

In the dream museum,
we see things that take
our breath away:

Paintings puncturing our being
again and again with joy. Wonder
squeezing us from inside out—

until hypoxia sets in. Until suffocation.
We don't die, of course.
We want to begin again.

We look up for help,
but a guard is adamant—
"No touching. Keep moving."

We hear feet shuffling past our ears,
and begin to be forever free
from all this joy-ending

not-breathing
forever.

The Cat In The Dream

The cat knows
my hand. I remember

songs sung through
wet rags,

the reading
of long dull poems,

and paintings turning
to pop-up puddles…

"I only remember your voice,"
says the cat. "I hide it in my fur,

and listen to it
during storms."

By dawn we were both hungry.
The sky was grumbling with rain.

There was a lot to forget.

Hard Prey In Green Winter

Sunny days in December.
More in January. Long thaws
and frost-free windows.
Who put summer here?
Did I forget to put it away?

———

"If it's not in your head,
it better be in your feet."
Who said that? My mother.
When? When I was young.
Before she died at age 98.

———

I hunt myself now without
a stopping place. Without
field glasses and a canteen.
I go room to room: Looking
for what? To get what?

———

My television can't remember
it was once black and white. I
ask for shows like Route 66,
Naked City, The Millionaire.
It doesn't respond. I forget why.

———

"Green winter, full graveyard."
Who said that? My grandmother.
When? Around 1918, to my dad
who would have been ten or eleven.
Years before she forgot his name.

———

When you die, do you take
your memories with you, or are
they left in a bed or a crashed car?
Will I forget everything
I've forgotten forever?

———

What do my empty hands
mean to do? What am I to
carry, or pick up, or take from
a shelf. Who can say?
Who will I ask?

———

I wish my carpet would turn
to snow. Wish I could track myself
room to room, like a rabbit in winter.

Poem Picks A Fight

Drunk, a poem picked a fight
with an unsuspecting reader.
Mocked her assertions
of tiredness. Laughed
at her growing disdain.

"We need to talk. You
need to listen" said the poem,
rolling up its long sleeves. Irrelevant
but nearby, a soccer stadium
erupted in cheers, just
as a child pulling a yellow
plastic wagon passed
between the reader
and the poem saying,
"there are no pagodas
in Bogotá. I checked."

What happened next
isn't clear. Maybe it was
just silence. Who knows?
How often things seem
astonishing, only to
dwindle down to not
surprising at all.

New Girl In Class

She could give answers
without raising her hand
or moving her lips.

At first, we resented
not being called on.
Later, we were grateful.

Each day, we wished
she wasn't real. Wished,
she would disappear.

Back home,
our report cards
were turning
a charcoal black

in the safes
our parents purchased
to hide them
from fire.

The Buboes (1347 - 1350)

Was it the mead or one deep breath in my sleep?
I wake up with this ache
I am all stench and ache

I have prayed and shrived
I have given half my herd
To the Holy Wench...

And now these buboes
Now my bed bulging
With the stench of me

Use Your Words

You must tell me
what you need to hear,

what clouds must
disappear from my face—

just who's back must never
turn on you. You must

use your words
before they get cold

or too old to remember
what they can do…

7:28 a.m. New Year's Day, 2021

7:28 a.m. New Year's Day. Dark.
Dark as it was at 7:28 p.m.

on New Year's Eve.

Out with the dark,
in with even more...

Back in Washington,
our president returns from golfing in Florida,

to continue his plan
to overthrow the first country

invented by sunlight.

All You Need To Know About That

A liar was elected president of a country.
He was unelected as soon as possible.
He says that's a lie.

Chinese Takeout Orders

Gorged on starches
And buzzed by salt,
Using flagpoles
Like giant chopsticks

A bulging mob marched
To stop a lawful eviction;
Their eyes glazed with
Saucy conviction.

For a bit, it looked like
The mob would taste
A victory worthy of
Zuo Zongtang—

The great General Tso himself...

But after three hours,
The salts and starches
Vanished from their guts.
Unsatisfied hunger

Renewed its presence;
As it always does with
Chinese takeout

And other *orders to go.*

Torn Yellow Sofa

On a lawn, someone
and someone else

are covering the defecation
of a dog with a torn yellow sofa.

It's precisely 3:08 p.m.
It's been raining since noon.

Tomorrow will be sunny.
Certainly tired feet will stop,

then go somewhere else.

Dusk To Dust

Friday. Home for the evening.
Wind in the leafless maples
near the driveway: tiny
noiseless movements.

Two lights on in the room
facing north. Dusk moves in
there, settles on the books,
and the piano and two mouths
speaking on a television.

Tomorrow is Saturday.
Company is coming.
There will be chores:
Carpets need vacuuming.
The table set at a new angle.

Dusk will return with guests.
We will toast each other from shining
glasses—while dusk moves slowly
through each room, touching surfaces
and faces, looking for dust.

Forthcoming

A book is forthcoming,
the musical made from it too.
In the opinion of the jury, a witness
was forthcoming.

The opposite of forthcoming
is withholding. Like a tax, or
a kind word. Or love itself.

The past. The present.
A truth. A love. Which one
will break the chains
of custody today?

The windows are open,
the breeze is tinctured
by scarves dipped in
hyacinth and lilac;

it's you—

Would That

There's not a ghost I can't properly greet.
Would that I were too young for all that.

Would that we would say what we mean
while we can remember what that is.

Would that our poems could read and live
like movies we couldn't get tickets to.

Would that we were all just tall enough
to see over every imaginary wall.

It Appears You Have Remained

We have received your resume
And curriculum of home studies.
The package of candied yams
And the pictures of your son's

Participation trophies are herewith.
We cannot accept such items.

It appears that you have remained
Age and weight appropriate
Although you are a former smoker.
Good for you!

Thank you for your interest
In this tiny fissure in the wall
Of dashed expectations.
You're obviously resilient.

Stages Of Life

1. College:
smoke and beers

2. Profession:
smoke and mirrors

3. Retirement:
spoken fears

Like That

Like that poem you get
to sit inside, not moving.

With the doors locked.
And the radio off.

With the big engine
of everything else,

turned off.

Like that.
Like, that.

The Trip Was Nothing
To Talk About

I took all the silences you created
and drove them to a rented house
in Maine, on the coast.

Thought: a summer vacation…
Falls are beautiful there…
Winters of famous poems…

The trip up was nothing to talk about
of course. We stared out of rolled-down windows,
and wondered what the future would be like.

When we arrived at the house,
it was darker than I expected.
For a moment, I questioned the whole idea.

But then we all went inside and found
rooms we could call our own—
it was just like home.

The rooms refreshed us.
We went to bed happy
to be sleeping alone.

Then you arrived.
And here we are.

Warning Codes And The Laughter Of Rain

The flashing yellow street light
the soft yellow rings
around a bumble bee

the yellow blotches
on a fire salamander
the yellow banded krait snake

the paper wasp
the hornet, the creamy yellows
of the taipan snake

the old yellow school bus
the new fire truck
the color-blind rain

falling for days
on heavy yellow
raincoats

laughing

The Yoga Of Rain

with thanks, to Pris

Yesterday, I turned from a window
and someone told me to smile. My face
suddenly went deaf. But I could
taste rain on my tongue.

―――――

Rain is always about tomorrow.
About growth. About thirst.
About ice. It forms puddles
that look for your face
trying to avoid them.

―――――

You want more than this dark wetness.
But you can't say what
that would be. It's not
the sun again.
It might be snow.
You never know.

―――――

Rain continues
its argument with the sun.
It cools the side of a face
curls in a leaf
intones a rhythm
on carports
from Southern Florida
to Bangor, Maine.

―――――

Today, rain fell on the dojo.
At the end of the yoga class, the guru
said imagine your face softened,
and staring up at you
from a puddle.

_____

Relax. Stare back. Smile.

Keep Moving

- For Rita at 60

Aging is a body
of ancient laws
at work. A process

of motions, and
objections thereof.
Sustained or overruled,

keep moving.
Do hard things.
Keep moving—

the cop's wrong.
There's *everything*
for you to see here.

Cup

The cup
feels my breath
leaving with a guest.

It remembers
the warmth
of two things.

Disabling "And Then"

First on the job, grammarians
with doughnuts, drinking coffee
smoking in late November air...

———

Next, a black pickup truck
piled high with lipstick tubes

pulled to the curb...

———

Last on the job, seagulls
pecking at pieces of boiled bread
left by sloppy bakers....

———

Next, next, next, next, next...

Desire

The waitress
leans in
and speaks

a garlic-infused
alphabet of
the day's specials.

Unable to
re-pronounce
one entree,

she writes:
"and one wants
my breath."

Choice Builds A Bungalow

Choice built a
little bungalow
next to my Will.

Waived at me
going to work.
Raked my leaves.

I would come home
to find my lawn mowed
and my cat fed.

My Will got fat.
Self-reliance was blunted
and soon failed.

I once stood for an hour
staring into a glass case
full of doughnuts.

Long lines formed
behind me yelling
threats and saying

"It's just a doughnut!"
"Pick one already!"
"Just pick one!"

Months passed.
Choice changed
its mind. Moved.

By then, frost had
formed on my Will.
Friends came with
coffee, pastry and
oranges. They sighed
at how my lawn,

gone gangrenous
with clover, would
need to be removed.

The Dead Poets Tour Of Minneapolis

Minneapolis
Minnesota

snow falling
and a slight wind

on the Washington
Avenue Bridge where

John Berryman is still busy
hurtling himself

into the western bank
of the Mississippi River,

where Robert Bly
sits, trying to turn

The Iliad
into a haiku,

and James Wright
lectures the homeless

on Sioux war cries
and hammocks.

Finally, we'll tour Fifth St. SE,
and Allen Tate's seminar

disparaging Allen Ginsberg
and praising Laura Riding

while making his wife
wait and wait for him
to locate where he put
their fugitive marriage

and newer New Criticism.

The Empty And Odorless Nature Of Language

The cat can't spell its own name.
But he doesn't think thoughts
like that in English. English isn't
something to fear or eat.

Emptiness makes all
cups similar. But thirsts vary.
Ask any student on the first
day of algebra class.

Words are the hear/see
of our world, but they
arrive and stay odorless.
They are an emptiness
to a cat. Meaningless.
Much like the way the word
"love" is repeated into nothingness
by the English-speaking world.

Emptiness is commonplace.
But thirsts vary.
Ask the clean plates,
the spotless mugs
in your cupboard.
Listen to all that
lack of language you
set the table with.

The earth won't turn on its axis
because it's told to. Words don't work
in outer space; vacuums can't vibrate.
Still, like a cat, it keeps coming around.

Eric Arthur Blair (1903 - 1950)

No christening of
Nor gravesite for
George Orwell

Has ever been found.

But Eric Arthur Blair
Swore that Orwell
Lived. Swore

Up to the moment
Of his death on
January 21, 1950...

Meaning forever.

Seeing The Eye Doctor

I told the doctor
"I can't see myself
Wearing glasses."

The exam continued.
We talked about High School
And California.

About forest fires
And her first husband
(Who died in an elevator).

At the right juncture
Of time and silence
I reiterated:

"I don't see myself
Wearing glasses."
"No one does,

No one can,
No one cares,"
She said;

And apologized
For the "depth"
Of her breath.

Later, emerging
From behind a machine,
She added,

"I'm sorry. I see
What you mean."

Commercials Love Poems

Commercials
Love poems

All the voices
All the colors

All the quick cuts
Between the world of desire

And the world of regret

Between wanting
And forgetting

Between all at once
And all for everyone

In just a few seconds

Another Poem Sleeping On The Wing

> The eyes roll asleep as if turned by the wind
> and the lids flutter open slightly like a wing.
> —Frank O'Hara

With a snort
he caught himself
sleeping

on the wing
of a plane. Unfortunately

no one could see
all his waving.
He was alone again.

The plane taxied
to takeoff. The runway
features blurred

as the wing brokered
the sky—"There's nothing
to do now but hold on

for as long as I can,"
he told himself…Then

"Maybe I'll just
fall asleep again.
Get all this falling

into a poem
by Frank O'Hara,
over for good."

Outside, crickets
practiced echolalia
on the only word they know.

Clouds moved sheepishly.

The moon yawned.

A wing and a poem
disappeared.

Two Four-Pound Notes

(I)

Outside of this poem, snow and memories
fall. Trees look in on you, like you were their
child. Like you need to be fed or burped.

In front, a Great Lake.
On the right, a Rocky River.
To the left, the absence of windows;
the unknown.

Nearby the halls are busy.
The elevators lift feet as far as they can.
Then, like your dad said: you're on your own.

You came to what you call "here" in 2005.
That was a year of changes. New job.
New home. One memory after another
falling like snow. And melting off-camera.

(II)

It's an hour before
the soup is done. There's a snow shovel
hanging in a garage you don't own anymore.
Someone takes it down, groaning, groaning.

Quacy. Query. Quential.
The French have built restaurants
in the English language! The one
the Irish were scourged to death with.

Inadequacies. Inquiries. Inconsequential efforts.
Neither the snow nor the trees speak
in words like that. They need no
tongue; no more than a window does.

Outside of this poem, non sequiturs roam the halls
knocking on doors for a new kind of salvation,
and a donation of two four-pound notes.

What Are We Watching And Who Can Hear Us?

Our choices are held
in a black magic wand
that we shake

at a hole in our lives.

There's nothing about your face
that told me where you were going.
Still, I took the seat next to yours.

And we watched a film together—forever.

I never see that couple anymore, but I know
they're in there. I knock, they just don't answer.
I hear a radio. I hear a cat.

Once, I heard Mozart.

I wish our lives came with subtitles.
You mistake my gestures. I whisper in metaphors.
Someone said that once.

Was it you?

———————

So what are we watching?
And who can hear us?
It's late. Just point to a hole,

and push.

A Phenomenology Of "Yes" And "No"

Wind says "yes"
to clouds, clouds
repeat the word
to rain. Ground
gulps it down
and plants
repeat it
in long
green
rows:

"yes"
"yes"
"yes"
"yes"
"yes"
"yes"
"yes"
…

There's
no such
echo
to "no."

The Reproductive System Of Words

Part One

All is metaphor
says the world in quotes
the world that flings us

forward and back
in and out of our
native tongue

in another voice, then another, and another...

_____

Well- worn words, bathe in mid-air
and arrive feeling fresh

a plant quotes a plant
and becomes a tree's long discussion

of barometric pressures
and the weight of sunlight
on early spring greens

slowly changing the meaning
of everything

_____

I don't see the tree above me
but it sees me down below

It sees me
looking for a tree, that particular tree,

and it smiles like a piny green ocean.
There's a word for that kind of joy

and a word for this...

———

Nothing stays put.....
For every "other" there's "another."
The reproductive system of words
is always on the hunt. Metaphors
and luck, *in vivo* Las Vegas

We become the shape
of a metaphor, blending
so well into our lives
we keep losing track of it

———

"That metaphor really becomes you.
Wherever did you find it?" "Nonsense,"
you say. "Over here" you say, pretending
to shake hands in a full-length mirror

———

On a kitchen stove, a pot calls a kettle black.
A kettle says "You run like a frying pan"
In a kitchen drawer, a fork
drew the winning hand

See? This is just what I mean. Metaphor.
And comedy reigns to keep us moist

———

More? After kissing, the couple decided to marry.
They had a few good years. But then ran out of words for each
other.
Later they shared photographs of metaphors to prove
they were once better than their current attention span.
See? There's no ending. Not with this.

———

Part Two

If a number is an abstract invisibility
and a numeral is a symbol of that vapor
and numerals can't be words,

Well then, only a metaphor can say one plus one
equals Jesus. Or Muhammad. Or Buddha.

Only a metaphor can come unto us,
to be us, to save us, to love and forgive us

———

Isn't it true? Isn't it wonderful? Me in the air,
and you laughing and rolling around
on the ground.

Well of course it is.

The spirit within us is also among us. In bottles
that are poured around the world. We need
to be cordial, they say, to be Irish or Scotch

or sit in a German garden made out of beer

———

We inhabit our latest metaphor
and spread ourselves out against a darkening sky
that would rather sleep than receive us.

We drink and wait, listening to Mendelssohn
and Meddlesome. We tackle better ways to hear
more and other. Then demand our ears explain themselves
using words without the fertility of notebooks

_____

Often off-key, but always pitch perfect, we rub our hands
with glee and sit down to 88 keys of metaphor or more.

Even though troubled air isn't concrete and
doesn't correlate, we eagerly hear where we are
for a short period of time. Then inhabit an abstract silence.

Later, we will hum as much metaphor as we can remember
while we make up the rest.

Afraid To Land

Before my memory
became a town
under bombardment

I stood on runways
waving to you
in your airplane

You would wave back
wearing orange gloves
and begin to descend...

Now there are holes
as far as the ear
can see and hear.

They say my paragraphs
are all out of order.

They keep me
off the tarmac.
I wait in a small room

for you to come
with photographs.

January Above The River

January. Confetti-sized snowflakes frisk around our twelve windows facing north. Six stories below, irregular and unconnected spots of ice have formed on the Rocky River: white jigsaw shapes on green water, like an enormous sea snake that has arrived from the depths of Lake Erie. My wife and I stare at its icy molting. Nearby, our cat cleans himself continuously. Perhaps he is preparing for the scentless stalking of this giant prey. Or perhaps he's attempting to make himself invisible.

Read This Slowly

Before you remember what you forgot
you were looking for somewhere else
In the space between what's done
and what is waiting to be done
Read this slowly like in first grade
the letters becoming syllables the syllables
becoming words, the words bringing out
the best in your mind that day
according to the pretty teacher
and giving you something
to talk about later
huddled around
the warmth of
the television.

I Need A Word With You

When you said, "I need
a word with you," I auditioned
dictionaries and chose one
no longer in print or online.

On arrival, your secretary,
who looked like a younger version
of your wife, offered me tea
and tangerines, in that order.

I immediately had doubts—
Words have so many relatives.
Meanings multiply and
and feelings are rarely spared.

I could hear you in your office.
You were upset about something
that involved tea and tangerines.
I handed a tiny piece of paper

to your wife-like secretary.
I left without saying a word.

The Worst Whatever Ever

Lines at the grocery store
the gas station
the hardware store.

If they're right, a snowstorm
2,000 miles long is going to
to take away our lights and our roads.

It's almost always an exaggeration.
The weather warms. The lake unfreezes.
The Worst Whatever Ever has to wait.

It's happened before: the school said
yes, the girl said yes, the doctor said
you're lucky…

We have food for three days
and good lanterns. More books
than we could read in 10 years.

Still, I'll buy a new snow shovel.
We'll go on that vacation. I'll get
a second opinion,

right after the storm.

Future Tense

The verb struggled
with its lack of sleep

with the tight shoes
that hurt its feet

through the night
from the previous day—

then put its arms
around the morning

with its promises
of coffee, eggs,

toast and sleep...

When?

When my salad days have
turned to feed corn. When my
thoughts are bundled, and drying
in fields made ready for winter.

When my hopes have lost
their proof, and drip in long
undistilled sentences for anyone
who returns my "hello."

That's when.

In The Capital Of The World

Troublemaker clouds
are blocking the sun's warmth

perforated for rain
putting out fires

we've been longing for
since summer

———

Here, I absorb the touch
of your gaze

like sea breeze
from glazed-green waves—

"Manhattan
is just another lake

churning at the speed of light,"
says someone walking behind me…

———

We'll end here, I think.
"Look at that," you say

Loose

Today we consider
the word "loose"
from the Latin word "laxus"
meaning "loose!"

This is what
the Romans would shout
at you, if your toga
went flapping

like a flag
around your body
on windy days
at the forum...

Later, the English,
who stole potatoes
large marbles
and whole cultures,
studied the toga,

and quietly folded it
into a pair of slacks.

Speaking Of The Dead

The deaf find
words and sounds
embedded
in their fingers.

——

Now is the time of wonder.

——

Objects hand
visions of time
and space
to the blind.

——

Will we continue
to speak to each other
inside our urn?

——

Or will we leave,
to learn the chironomy
of the extinct?

——

Now is the time to wonder.

217

Buried In The Gaps

"What we can't bear we bury." —David Young

1.
You are the gap
dug into my memory—
you, book

and you, film
but most of all
it was your face

at your brother's funeral…

"What we can't bear,
we bury," said a poet,
handing me a shovel
and a bottle of gin.

2.
The harder I try to remember
the more the air smells
like fresh earth, until

something else presents
me with a piece of paper
and a pen, saying "Sign
here, and here."

No, I can't find the book.
No, I can't remember the name
of the film (but I remember
every frame). Yes, her face.

Signed—me. And—me.

3.
Today I looked
at early photos
of us as Us,

replicas of being and time
that will never declare
what we couldn't bear

or where we are buried.

ABOUT THE AUTHOR

---◆◎◆---

Timothy Donohue is the author of three books of poetry and co-author of one. In a professional career spanning four decades, he spent the first 20 years as a writer, producer and sometimes teacher of print and broadcast advertising. He spent the following 20 years as a managing administrator and Communications Director for non-profits dedicated to providing services to individuals with mental illness, developmental disabilities and chemical dependencies. He realized over time, that poetry could quit him any time it wanted to, but he couldn't quit poetry no matter what he did.

Made in the USA
Middletown, DE
05 October 2022

11881676R00129